Jewelry & Accessories
from Everyday Objects

Jewelry & Accessories
from Everyday Objects

19 Unique Projects

Inspired by Found Objects

and Ready-Made Materials

Tair Parnes

Creative Publishing international

Creative Publishing
international

First published in 2007 by
Creative Publishing international, Inc.
18705 Lake Drive East
Chanhassen, Minnesota 55317
1-800-328-3895
www.creativepub.com
All rights reserved

President/CEO: Ken Fund
VP Sales & Marketing: Peter Ackroyd
Executive Managing Editor: Barbara Harold
Creative Director: Michele Lanci-Altomare
Design Manager: Jon Simpson
Production Managers: Laura Hokkanen, Linda Halls
Design: Eddie Goldfine
Photography: Danya Weiner
Editor: Shoshana Brickman
Layout: Gala Pre Press Ltd.

Copyright 2007 Penn Publishing Ltd.

Printed in China
10 9 8 7 6 5 4 3 2 1

Library of Congress Cataloging-in-Publication Data

Parnes, Tair
  Jewelry & accessories from everyday objects : 19 unique projects inspired by found objects and ready-made materials / Tair Parnes.
    p. cm.
ISBN-13: 978-1-58923-327-0 (soft cover)
ISBN-10: 1-58923-327-1 (soft cover)
  1. Handicraft. 2. Jewelry making. 3. Found objects (Art) I. Title.
II. Title: Jewelry and accessories from everyday objects.

TT157.P3137 2007
745.594'2--dc22   2007003470

CONTENTS

INTRODUCTION 6

How to Use This Book **6**

About the Author **6**

MATERIALS 7

Ready-Made Components **7**

Standard Materials **8**

TOOLS 9

JEWELRY 10

Beauty and the Butterfly Bracelet **12**

Merriest Mini Ornament Bracelet **16**

Tinkling Golden Nib Bracelet **20**

Old Macdonald's Preferred Pearl Earrings **24**

Fly-By-Night Lure Earrings **30**

Catch-Me-If-You-Can Lure Necklace **36**

Alluring Lure Necklace **42**

Fanciful Floral Collar **48**

Funny Bunny Ring **52**

Sealed with a Kiss Stamp Necklace **56**

Philatelist's Favorite Brooch **62**

Bouquet of Buttons Brooch **68**

Twinkling Wreath Brooch **72**

ACCESSORIES 76

Madame Butterfly's Hair Comb **78**

Jingle-Jangle Coin Belt **82**

Hip-Hugging Safety Pin Belt **88**

I'll Drink to That! Handbag Charm **94**

Button-Up-The-Evening Bag **100**

Zipper-A-Dee-Doo-Dah Purse **106**

INTRODUCTION

Everyone has quirky treasures lying around their house—items that have outlived their usefulness, but simply can't be thrown away. These riches are often stored in shoeboxes and bags, tucked away in cupboards and closets. We can't bear to part with them, but we don't know exactly what to do with them, either. More often than not, they simply end up gathering dust in a corner, only to be discovered during spring cleaning, looked at nostalgically, then packed away again.

With *Jewelry & Accessories: 19 Unique Projects Inspired by Found Objects and Ready-Made Materials* in hand, you can bring these treasures to life in a creative new guise. You'll find instructions for 19 projects using a variety of common materials in a range of uncommon contexts. Miniature animals become delicate dangling earrings; fountain pen nibs are transformed into tinkling bracelet charms; cat-shaped chocolate molds are incorporated into colorful brooches. All of the Ready-Made components in these projects are kept intact—their form stays the same while their function is changed. The bottle caps in **I'll Drink to That! Handbag Charm** (page 94), they're not capping bottles, but that doesn't mean people won't recognize them for what they are. What makes each of these projects so distinct is the everyday-ness of its primary components!

How to Use this Book

No two people have the same assortment of collected treasures. Although each project comes with a detailed description of the Ready-Made components I used—and advice on where to buy them—don't feel constrained by these guidelines. To the contrary! Be encouraged and inspired to make substitutions that suit you, and to find the artistic element hiding in the everyday objects that surround you.

About the Author

Tair Parnes is one of Tel Aviv's most exciting fashion designers. Inspired by vibrant colors and international influences, she excels at taking everyday items and turning them into remarkable objects of art. Tair has studied a wide range of art forms, from classic art and curatorship to weaving and working with gold. In addition to designing clothing, tapestries, and jewelry, Tair instructs people of all ages in the field of art appreciation, and teaches occupational therapy. In *Jewelry & Accessories: 19 Unique Projects Inspired by Found Objects and Ready-Made Materials,* Tair transforms hum-drum household items into works of art by altering their function without making significant changes to their form. For any reader who has ever saved anything with the hope of putting it to good use one day—this is a book worth saving (and using!).

MATERIALS

Ready-Made Components

The inspiration for these projects came from materials I found around my home. Your home has its own Ready-Made components waiting to be discovered—here are some hints on where to find them:

Kitchen Accessories

Kitchen cupboards and drawers are excellent sources for finding a world of Ready-Made materials. I've used **cupcake liners**, **chocolate molds**, **chocolate wrappers**, and **bottle caps** in these projects. Look around your kitchen closely—I'm sure you'll find lots of items that would look simply delicious dangling from a chain or pinned onto a brooch.

Office Supplies

Everyone has office supplies cluttering up their desk drawers. Some people even have home offices—these offer a plethora of potential ideas. In the following pages, you'll find projects that include **roundhead fasteners** and **fountain pen nibs**. Rummage through some of the drawers in your desk—you'll be amazed at what you come up with.

Party Favors

It's a shame to save **colorful ribbons** and **bright balloons** only for special events. Ready-Made is a great chance for integrating festive party favors into jewelry and accessories all year long, and without waiting for an occasion to celebrate! These projects will get you thinking twice before throwing away **wrapping paper** and the like, as their potential may extend far beyond a single celebration!

Seasonal Specialties

Everyone loves holidays, and most holidays today come with a variety of festive ornaments and decorations. I've integrated **miniature Christmas bells**, and **tree ornaments** into these projects. Think of your favorite seasonal decorations and use them in a Ready-Made project of your own. This way you can show them off all year long, and in every season!

Sewing Kit

Even households that don't have any professional sewers have some sort of First Aid Kit for mending. These projects use sewing staples such as **zippers**, **safety pins**, and **buttons** in unconventional manners. They also use leftover pieces of fabric and well-worn jeans.

Stamps, Coins, and other Collectibles

There is no need to limit your Ready-Made explorations to your own collections—peruse (with permission) the assorted collections of your family and friends to find wide-ranging items waiting to be transformed into art. **Stamps**, **coins**, **miniature figures**, **fishing lures**, and **stickers** are integrated into these projects. Drill holes and string them on jump rings to convert these collectibles into unique (and charming) charms.

In addition to Ready-Made components, the projects in this book require some standard materials as well. Most of these can be found at bead stores and hobby shops; a vast selection is available online. Feel free to adapt and substitute materials in every project with the colors, sizes, and styles you prefer.

Beads

I love beads. I love big beads and small beads, seed beads and pearl beads, smooth beads and textured beads. Choose the beads for each project according to your favorite styles, shapes, and colors.

Chains

In most cases, you'll need to use a chain that has links to support jump rings. It doesn't matter what style of chain you choose, just check that your jump rings fit through the links. You'll also want to make sure the chain you choose isn't too heavy (or delicate) for the Ready-Made items you want to display.

Jewelry Findings

Jump rings, ear wires, headpins, eye pins, pinbacks, crimp beads, and clasps are all classified under this general category. They are used to string, connect, secure, and finish your project. Jewelry findings are usually available in gold, silver, or copper. Be sure to use excellent quality findings, as the life of your creation depends on them.

Fabric and Thread

Some of these projects require fabric and ribbons, tassels and thread. You may be able to use leftover fabric from other projects, or scraps of old clothing. As for threads, you may need sewing thread, beading thread, or embroidery floss.

Miscellaneous

Many of the materials you'll need for these projects are probably lying around your house—you just have to go find them. **Superglue** is used for pasting pinbacks to the back of brooches. **Gluesticks** are used for temporarily sticking objects before running them through the laminator. **Permanent markers** are used for marking the entry point for drilling. **Laminating pouches** are used for preparing stickers, stamps and other materials for lamination.

TOOLS

An **awl** is used to punch holes in laminated materials such as stamps and stickers. Be sure to use an awl with a thin point to make particularly tiny holes.

A **drill** and **drill bits** are used to drill holes in plastic figures and miniature lights. Use the smallest drill bit you can find and drill with care, as some of the objects you'll be drilling are likely quite delicate.

Flat-nose pliers give you an extra pair of fingers. To open a jump ring, hold one set of pliers in each hand and grasp both ends of the jump ring. Position the ring so that you see through the hole. Draw one pair of pliers toward you and push the other pair away. To close the ring, draw the pliers back to their original position. Flat-nose pliers can also be used to hold jump rings steady while inserting them into holes, and to mash crimp beads.

A **laminator** is used to laminate stickers, stamps, and other materials. Home laminators are available at office supply stores and some department stores. You can also prepare your materials for lamination at home, and bring them to a copy shop for laminating.

Needles of various styles are used in these projects. Beading needles are used to string beads—they have particularly thin eyes. Sewing needles are used to sew seams together; if you have a sewing machine, use it to save time. Embroidery needles are used for sewing decorative seams.

Round-nose pliers have round ends and are used to make loops in eye pins and headpins.

Scissors are used for cutting laminated items, thread, and fabric. Don't use scissors to cut wire, as this can ruin the scissors.

Wire cutters are used to cut wire, chains, headpins, and eye pins. If you are cutting a particularly thick chain, try opening the links instead of cutting them.

JEWELRY

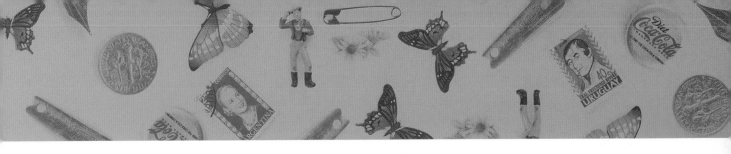

BEAUTY
AND THE BUTTERFLY
BRACELET

My daughter went through an intense butterfly phase, during which time her room (and our house) seemed to be literally fluttering with them. Though the phase ended eventually, our house still has more Monarch, Swallowtail, and Buckeye butterflies than most conservatories!

Ready-Made Component

Craft stores, toy stores, stationery stores, and office supply stores are all well stocked with **stickers** these days. Stores that sell supplies to nursery and primary school teachers usually have a wide selection of butterfly stickers, as these are a traditional favorite among young people.

13

4. Punch a hole in the center of a butterfly. Gently fold the butterfly in half along the body, so that the wings bend upward. Draw a jump ring through the hole.

5. Repeat Step 4 to prepare all of the butterflies.

MATERIALS

30 butterfly stickers

Lamination pouch

32 silver jump rings, 1/4" (0.6 cm) in diameter

Silver chain, 7" (17.8 cm) in length

Silver lobster clasp

Laminator

Scissors

Awl

2 flat-nose pliers

INSTRUCTIONS

1. Arrange the stickers in a random fashion in the lamination pouch. Make sure the stickers aren't too close together.

2. Laminate the stickers using a home or industrial laminator.

3. Cut out the laminated stickers. Leave a margin of 1/8" (0.3 cm) around each one so that the lamination doesn't separate.

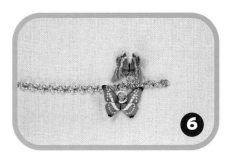

6. Attach a butterfly from Step 5 to a link in the chain. Close the jump ring securely. Attach another butterfly to the chain so that the two butterflies are close together.

7. Repeat Step 6 until the bracelet is brimming with butterflies. To finish, attach jump rings to both ends of the chain and attach the clasp to one of the jump rings.

MERRIEST MINI
ORNAMENT
BRACELET

Is there anyone who doesn't love Christmas ornaments? And though decorating a tree is one way of using them, it's certainly not the only one. This bracelet is a great way to show off miniature ornaments and bring a handful of holiday cheer with you everywhere you go!

Ready-Made Component

When the season is right, **Christmas ornaments** can be found everywhere. Miniature ornaments may be a little harder to find, but craft stores, gift stores, and specialty stores generally have a good supply on hand. The Internet is a good source for finding miniature ornaments all year long.

MATERIALS

3 plaid bows

23 miniature Christmas ornaments, 3/4" (2 cm) in length

28 copper jump rings, 1/8" (0.3 cm) in diameter

Copper chain, 14" (36 cm) in length

Copper lobster clasp

2 flat-nose pliers

Wire cutters

INSTRUCTIONS

1. Attach a jump ring to each of the plaid bows.

2. Attach a jump ring to each of the Christmas ornaments.

3. Cut the chain in half so that you have 2 chains, each measuring 7" (18 cm) in length.

4. Attach an ornament to one of the chains.

5. Repeat Step 4 to attach 12 more ornaments to the chain.

6. Attach the remaining ornaments and the bows to the other chain.

7. Connect the chains by attaching jump rings at both ends.

8. To finish, attach the clasp to one end of the bracelet.

TINKLING GOLDEN NIB
BRACELET

My mother bought a package of 100 gold fountain pen nibs at a flea market in Argentina about 30 years ago. The nibs are excellent for sketching and calligraphy, and although I used several as intended, tens of them sat in their box untouched until I turned them into these tinkling charms.

Ready-Made Component

Fountain pen nibs can be found at art supply stores and specialty pen shops. Make sure the nibs you choose have a hole at the flat end for stringing them onto jump rings. You'll need to select the width of your jump rings according to the size of the hole, so I suggest bringing one of the nibs with you when buying jump rings to make sure they fit.

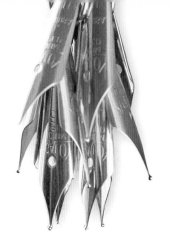

MATERIALS

50 gold fountain pen nibs, with holes at either end 26 gold jump rings, ¼" (0.6 cm) in diameter

Gold lobster clasp

2 flat-nose pliers

INSTRUCTIONS

1. Open a jump ring, string on 2 nibs, and close the jump ring.

2. Open another jump ring. String a nib, the jump ring from Step 1, and another nib. Close the jump ring.

3. Open another jump ring. String a nib, the jump ring from Step 2, and another nib. Close the jump ring.

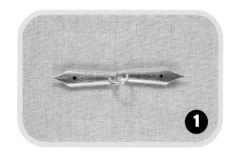

4. Repeat Step 3 to make a chain of jump rings and nibs. Measure the chain as you work, and continue attaching jump rings and nibs until it fits comfortably around your wrist.

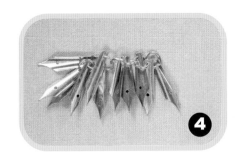

5. To finish, attach a second jump ring to the last jump ring and attach the clasp to the first jump ring.

OLD MACDONALD'S
PREFERRED PEARL
EARRINGS

As the mother of three sons, chances were good that one of them would be crazy about model train sets. But who would have thought all three of them would be?! With dozens of miniature animals and people, I didn't think anyone would notice if I borrowed a few pieces.

Ready-Made Component

Miniature animals are sold as accessories for train sets and dollhouses. Architects often use them in small-scale building models. Miniature figures of all types are sold in hobby shops and toy stores that specialize in collectibles, as well as art supply shops that cater to architects. Be sure to use animals that are plastic, since you'll have to drill a hole through the center.

MATERIALS

2 miniature zebras, 1/2" (1.3 cm) in length

4 miniature cows, 1/2" (1.3 cm) in length

6 freshwater pearl beads, 1/4" (0.6 cm) in diameter

12 silver headpins, 3/4" (1.9 cm) in length

12 silver jump rings, 1/5" (0.5 cm) in diameter

2 pieces of silver chain, each 2" (5 cm) in length

Pair of silver ear wires

Drill and #60 (1 mm) drill bit

Round-nose pliers

Wire cutters

2 flat-nose pliers

INSTRUCTIONS

1. Carefully drill a hole vertically in the middle of each animal.

2. String a pearl bead onto a headpin. Form a loop in the headpin and trim any excess wire. Attach a jump ring to the loop.

3. Repeat Step 2 to string all of the pearl beads onto headpins and attach jump rings.

4. String a zebra onto a headpin so that the head of the pin is under the zebra's belly. Form a loop in the headpin and trim any excess wire. Attach a jump ring to the loop.

5. Repeat Step 4 to string all of the animals onto headpins and attach jump rings.

6. Attach a cow to the bottom link in one of the chains.

7. Attach a zebra to a link in the chain that is about 1/2" (1.3 cm) above the cow.

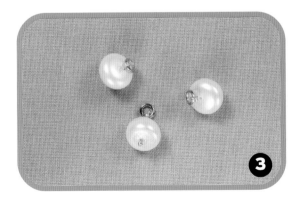

8. Attach 2 pearl beads to a link in the chain that is about 1/2" (1.3 cm) above the zebra.

9. Attach a pearl bead to a link in the chain that is about 1/4" (0.6 cm) above the pearl beads you attached in Step 8.

10. Attach another cow to a link in the chain that is about 1/4" (0.6 cm) from the single pearl bead.

11. Attach an ear wire to the topmost link in the chain.

12. Repeat Steps 6 to 11 to make the other earring.

FLY-BY-NIGHT LURE
EARRINGS

My brother-in-law is an angler with a sense of style; he loves finding striking fish lures almost as much as he loves spending the weekend in his boat, waiting for the fish to bite. I grabbed these lures out of his tackle box when he wasn't looking. Once he saw the earrings they inspired, he asked me to make a matching necklace for my sister (see **Catch-Me-If-You-Can Lure Necklace**, page 34).

Ready-Made Component

Fly lures can be found in tackle shops and sporting goods stores. There are also plenty of specialty shops located in and around major fishing areas. Some anglers prefer making their fly lures by hand. If you go this route, there's no need to remove the hooks before turning the lures into jewelry—just leave them off to begin with!

MATERIALS

Pair of colorful fly lures,
2" (5 cm) in length

2 round red glass beads,
1/4" (0.6 cm) in diameter

8 seed beads, size 8°,
various colors

2 round orange glass beads,
1/4" (0.6 cm) in diameter

2 round yellow glass beads,
1/4" (0.6 cm) in diameter

4 round blue glass beads,
1/4" (0.6 cm) in diameter

2 silver eye pins, 3/4" (1.9 cm)
in length

10 silver headpins, 3/4" (1.9 cm)
in length

10 silver jump rings

2 pieces of silver chain, each 3/4"
(1.9 cm) in length

Pair of silver ear wires

Wire cutters

2 flat-nose pliers

INSTRUCTIONS

1. Remove the hook from a lure. Do this carefully, as the hook is sharp!

2. Open the loop in an eye pin, string on the lure, and close the loop.

3. String a red bead onto the shank of the eye pin. Make a loop in the eye pin and trim any excess wire. Attach a jump ring to the loop.

4. String a seed bead and an orange glass bead onto a headpin. Make a loop in the headpin and trim any excess wire. Attach a jump ring to the loop.

5. Repeat Step 4 to string 1 yellow and 2 blue glass beads onto headpins.

6. Attach the orange bead and yellow bead to the second link in one of the chains.

7. Attach the blue beads to the next link in the chain.

8. Attach the eye pin from Step 3 to the next link in the chain.

9. Attach the ear wire to the top link in the chain.

10. Repeat Steps 1 to 9 to make the second earring.

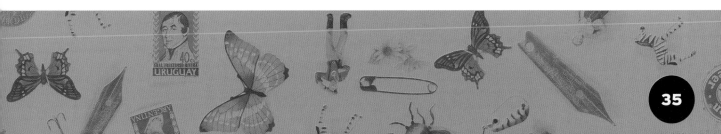

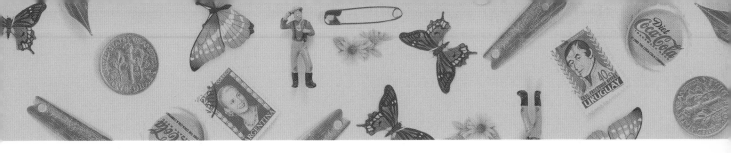

CATCH-ME-IF-YOU-CAN LURE
NECKLACE

When my brother-in-law asked me to make a necklace for my sister with fish lures, I knew it had to be special. That's why I integrated freshwater pearl beads in the design. The pearls contrast marvelously with the lures, both in terms of color and texture. I used five pairs of lures for symmetry, but using ten different lures creates a lovely random effect.

Ready-Made Component

Some avid anglers insist on making their own **fly lures**. They follow time-tested techniques, and buy specialty feathers and other materials. You can go this route, or pick up some ready-made fly lures at a tackle shop or sporting goods store.

MATERIALS

24 seed beads, size 8°, red, pink, and purple

12 glass beads, various sizes and colors

5 pairs of fly lures, various sizes and colors

8 round orange beads, 1/4" (0.6 cm) in diameter

44 freshwater pearl beads, 1/4" (0.6 cm) in diameter

20 silver jump rings, 1/4" (0.6 cm) in diameter

10 silver headpins, 1" (2.5 cm) in length

Beading thread

Silver hook and eye clasp

Wire cutters

2 flat-nose pliers
Round-nose pliers
Beading needle

INSTRUCTIONS

1. String a seed bead and a glass bead onto a headpin. Make a loop in the headpin and trim any excess wire. Attach a jump ring to the loop.

2. Repeat Step 1 to decorate all of the headpins.

3. Remove the hook from a lure. Do this carefully, as the hook is sharp! Attach a jump ring to the ring upon which the hook was suspended.

4. Repeat Step 3 to prepare all of the lures.

5. Thread the needle with a 47" (120 cm) piece of thread. Fold the thread in half and tie the ends together.

6. String 7 purple seed beads onto the thread. Draw the thread through the loop in the clasp, then draw back through the first seed bead to form a loop of beads around the clasp. Tie the ends of the string together in a secure double knot.

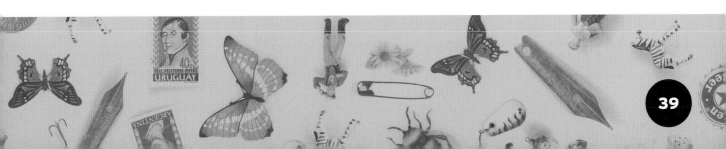

7. String a glass bead, 4 orange beads and 3 pearl beads.

8. String a decorated headpin and 2 pearl beads. String a lure and 2 pearl beads.

9. Repeat Step 8 another 4 times.

10. String a lure and 2 pearl beads. String a decorated headpin and 2 pearl beads.

11. Repeat Step 10 another 4 times.

12. String a pearl bead, 4 orange beads, and a glass bead.

13. String 7 purple seed beads. Draw the needle through the second part of the clasp, then draw back through the first seed bead to form a loop of beads around the clasp. Pull the string firmly to secure the clasp and tie in double knot.

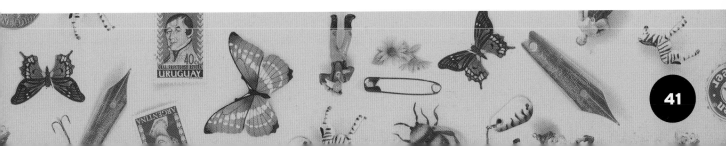

ALLURING LURE
NECKLACE

The lures in this necklace are called wobblers because they wobble when immersed in water, mimicking the motion of real fish. While some wobblers are better than others for catching fish, the deciding factor when it comes to making jewelry is wholly aesthetic. I chose these lures because I like their vibrant colors.

Ready-Made Component

You can find **wobbler lures** at sporting goods stores and tackle shops. If you're planning a trip to an area that has lots of fishing opportunities, look for hand-painted varieties in local specialty shops.

MATERIALS

25 wobbler lures

27 silver jump rings, ¼" (0.6 cm)
in diameter

Silver chain, 24" (61 cm)
in length

Silver lobster clasp

2 flat-nose pliers

INSTRUCTIONS

1. Remove the hook from a lure. Do this carefully, as the hook is sharp! Don't remove the ring upon which the hook was suspended.

2. Repeat Step 1 to remove hooks from all of the lures.

3. Attach a jump ring to the loop on the other end of the lure.

4. Repeat Step 3 to attach jump rings to all of the lures.

5. Find the middle of the chain (folding it in half is the easiest way of doing this) and attach a lure.

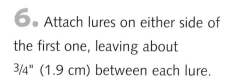

6. Attach lures on either side of the first one, leaving about 3/4" (1.9 cm) between each lure.

7. Continue attaching lures in this manner, checking periodically to make sure the necklace is symmetrical, until there is about 4" (10 cm) of chain left on each end.

8. To finish, attach jump rings to both ends of the chain and attach the clasp to one of the jump rings.

FANCIFUL FLORAL
COLLAR

Most households that have kids have a stash of stickers. Stickers are great for giving as token gifts, and for keeping young people busy on rainy days. Personally, I like having stickers on hand for decorating gifts, cards, and letters.

Ready-Made Component

Stickers are sold almost everywhere these days. Craft stores, toy stores, stationery stores, and office supply stores all provide thousands of adhesive options. I chose roses and butterflies for this necklace, but you can choose any motif you like.

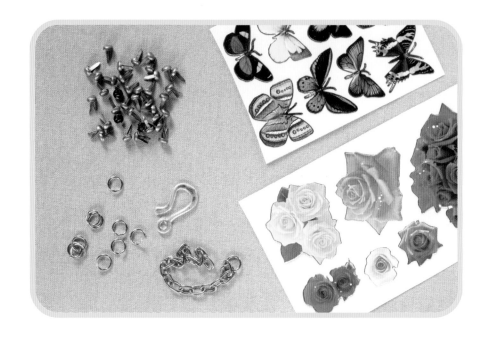

MATERIALS

50 flower stickers

5 butterfly stickers

60 roundhead fasteners, 1/2" (1.3 cm) shank

Lamination pouch

3 jump rings, 1/4" (0.6 cm) in diameter

2 pieces of silver chain, 2" (5 cm) and 5" (12.8 cm) in length

Silver hook and eye clasp

Laminator
Scissors
Awl
2 flat-nose pliers

INSTRUCTIONS

1. Arrange the stickers in a random fashion in the lamination pouch. Make sure the stickers aren't too close together.

2. Laminate the stickers using a home or industrial laminator.

3. Cut out the laminated stickers. Leave a 1/8 " (0.3 cm) margin around each sticker so that the lamination doesn't separate.

4. Punch holes in 2 stickers near their margins and connect with a fastener.

5. Punch another hole in one of the stickers you connected in Step 4. Punch a hole in a third sticker and connect the stickers with a fastener.

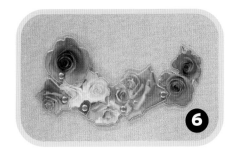

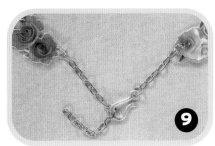

6. Continue connecting stickers in this manner to form a rounded collar shape. You'll want the necklace to be wider in the center than near the ends, so that the collar fits nicely around your neck.

7. Measure the necklace against your neck as you go, and stop attaching stickers when there is a gap of about 4" (10 cm) between the beginning and the end of the necklace.

8. Punch holes at both ends of the necklace and attach jump rings to each of the holes.

9. Attach the chains to the jump rings. Attach a jump ring to the end of the shorter chain and attach the clasp to the jump ring.

FUNNY BUNNY
RING

People will be hip-hopping over to see this playful ring. Cheerful and cute, it's everything a little bunny ring should be. Use pearly pink and white beads to make this ring particularly spring-themed.

Ready-Made Components

Miniature animals are sold as accessories for dollhouses. The **rabbit** in this piece was always a favorite, simply because it was so cute! **Miniature rabbits** are also abundant during the spring, when Easter decorations are widely available.

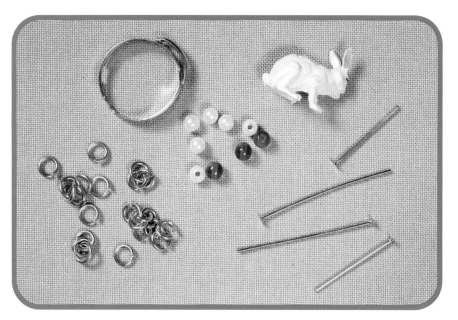

INSTRUCTIONS

1. String a bead onto a headpin. Form a loop in the headpin and trim any excess wire. Repeat to string all of the beads onto headpins.

2. Attach 6 beads to a jump ring, using a combination of pink and white beads. Close the jump ring.

3. Repeat Step 2 to string all of the beads onto jump rings.

4. Carefully drill a hole vertically in the middle of the rabbit.

MATERIALS

28 white plastic beads, 1/8" (0.3 cm) in diameter

8 pink plastic beads, 1/8" (0.3 cm) in diameter

Miniature rabbit, 1/2" (1.3 cm) in length

Silver charm ring base

36 headpins, 1/2" (1.3 cm) in length

7 silver jump rings, 1/5" (0.5 cm) in diameter

1 headpin, 3/4" (2 cm) in length

Wire cutters
Round-nose pliers
2 flat-nose pliers
Drill and #60 (1 mm) drill bit

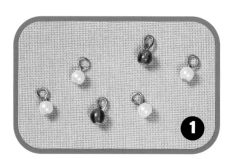

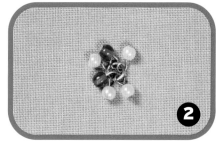

5. String the rabbit onto a headpin so that the head of the pin is flush against the rabbit's back. Form a loop in the headpin directly under the belly and trim any excess wire. Attach a jump ring to the loop.

6. Attach a jump ring with beads to the loop in the ring.

7. Repeat Step 6 to attach all of the beads to the ring.

8. To finish, attach the rabbit to the ring.

SEALED WITH A KISS
STAMP NECKLACE

I've been saving stamps since I was a child—this necklace gives me a chance to show off some of my favorites. As for the chocolate wrappers, I consider them to be miniature works of art in their own right. When good friends bring me confectionaries, they know I pay more attention to the wrappers than to the candies inside.

Ready-Made Components

You can find lots of special edition **postage stamps** at your local post office. If you know anyone who lives overseas, ask them to send you a letter with an attractive stamp or two. As for the **shiny wrappers**, eating fine chocolates is the tastiest way of getting these. For a lower-fat option, try reusing wrapping paper from presents you've given or received.

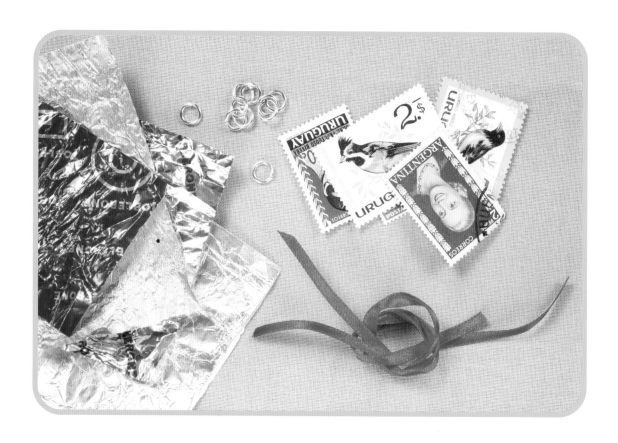

MATERIALS

13 shiny chocolate wrappers

13 postage stamps

14 silver jump rings, ¼" (0.6 cm) in diameter

Thin satin ribbon, red, 20" (50 cm) in length

Lamination pouch

Gluestick

Superglue

Scissors

2 flat-nose pliers

Laminator

Awl

INSTRUCTIONS

1. Flatten a wrapper so that the prettiest side faces upward. Spread a little glue on the back of a stamp and lay on the wrapper, pressing evenly to stick.

2. Cut the wrapper around the stamp, leaving a thin margin on all sides. You can leave an even margin around all sides, or make each margin a little different.

3. Repeat Steps 1 and 2 to mount all of the stamps on wrappers and trim.

4. Arrange the stamps in a random fashion in the lamination pouch. Make sure the stamps aren't too close together.

5. Laminate using a home or industrial laminator.

6. Cut out the laminated stamps. Leave a margin of 1/8" (0.3 cm) around each stamp so that the lamination doesn't separate.

7. Punch small holes on the top left and right corners of each stamp.

8. Draw a jump ring through both holes in one of the stamps. Close one of the jump rings securely, but leave the other ring slightly open.

3

8

9. String a second stamp onto the open jump ring then close the jump ring securely. Draw a jump ring through the other hole in the stamp, attach another stamp to the jump ring, and close the jump ring securely. Draw a jump ring through the other hole in the third stamp and leave slightly open.

10. Repeat Step 9 until all of the stamps are connected. Make sure the jump rings on either end of the chain are closed securely.

11. Cut the ribbon in half. Tie one half on the first jump ring with a double knot. Tie the other half on the last jump ring with a double knot. Secure both knots with drops of superglue.

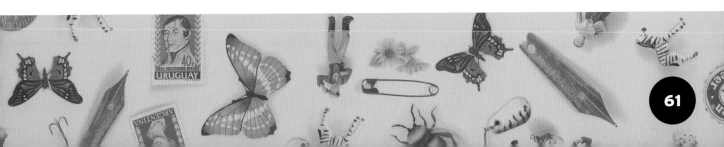

PHILATELIST'S FAVORITE
BROOCH

Finally! I found a use for all those stamps I've been saving! True, this brooch just uses a single stamp (see **Sealed with a Kiss Necklace** on page 54 for another stamp-based project) but I had to start somewhere. As for the figures, I borrowed a few from my son's model train set. I'm sure he'll never notice....

Ready-Made Components

Back in the days when mail was sent only by post, almost everyone collected **postage stamps**. Though letters are rarer today than in the past, postage stamps are far from obsolete. Find special edition stamps at your local post office; if you know anyone who lives overseas, you can ask them to send some snail mail. As for the **miniature figures**, they can be found in hobby shops and toy stores that specialize in collectibles, as well as art supply shops that cater to architects.

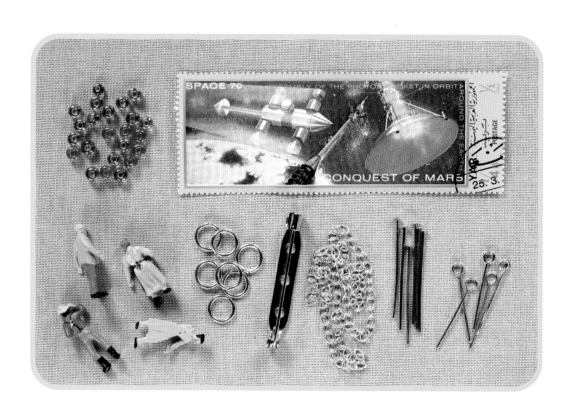

MATERIALS

Postage stamp, 4$^{1/2}$" (9 cm) in width

8 miniature figures

12 seed beads, size 6°, various colors

Silver pinback

8 silver headpins, $^{1/2}$" (1.3 cm) in length

12 silver eye pins, $^{1/2}$" (1.3 cm) in length

6 silver jump rings, $^{1/4}$" (0.6 cm) in diameter

Delicate silver chain, 11$^{1/2}$" (29.4 cm) in length

Lamination pouch

Superglue

Laminator

Scissors

Awl

Drill and #60 (1 mm) drill bit

Wire cutters

Round-nose pliers

2 flat-nose pliers

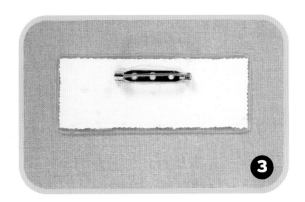

3

INSTRUCTIONS

1. Place the stamp in the lamination pouch and laminate using a home or industrial laminator.

2. Trim around the laminated stamp, leaving a margin of 1/8" (0.3 cm) so that the lamination doesn't separate.

3. Glue the pinback to the back of the stamp.

4. Punch 6 evenly spaced holes along the bottom of the stamp.

5. Carefully drill a hole horizontally through the middle of a figure. Draw a headpin through the hole so that the head of the pin is on the front of the figure. Form a loop in the headpin and cut any excess wire.

6. Repeat Step 5 to prepare all of the figures.

7. String a bead onto an eye pin and form a loop in the eye pin. Trim any excess wire.

8. Repeat Step 7 to string all of the beads onto eye pins.

9. Cut the chain into 14 pieces, 6 pieces measuring 1 1/4" (3.2 cm) and 8 pieces measuring 1/2" (1.3 cm).

10. Attach a figure to each of long chains.

11. Attach the remaining figures to 2 short chains.

6

17. Repeat Step 16 with the remaining beads and figures.

18. Attach a jump ring supporting beads and a figure to a hole in the stamp.

12. Attach 6 beads to jump rings.

19. Repeat Step 18 to attach all of the jump rings to the stamp.

13. Attach the remaining 6 beads to short chains.

14. Attach a long chain with a figure and a short chain with a bead to one of the beads with a jump ring.

15. Repeat Step 14 another 3 times.

16. Attach a long chain with a figure, a short chain with a bead, and a short chain with a figure to one of the beads with a jump ring.

BOUQUET OF BUTTONS
BROOCH

Take a close look at the buttons on your clothes—you may be surprised at the treasures you find. The simplest cotton blouse or plainest plaid shirt may have the most delicate array of buttons, just waiting to be 'borrowed' for another project.

Ready-Made Components

These **flowery buttons** were on a favorite blouse I wore for years. Though I eventually grew tired of the blouse, I simply couldn't part with the **buttons**. They were so dainty and elegant. As for the **plastic leaves**, these were part of an arrangement my grandmother kept for years on her mantle piece.

INSTRUCTIONS

1. Cut 12 pieces of wire of varying lengths, measuring between 2" (5 cm) and 4¹/2" (11.4 cm).

2. Glue a seed bead to one end of each wire.

3. String a crimp bead onto the other end of the wire. Draw it along for about ¹/4" (0.6 cm), leaving enough room for the tail of the wire to be drawn through another hole in the button. Mash the crimp bead with the flat-nose pliers.

4. String a button onto the tail of the wire. Draw the button until it meets the crimp bead, then bend the end of the wire through another hole in the button.

5. String another crimp beads onto the wire and draw it up to the button. Mash the crimp bead to secure it flush against the button, and trim any excess wire.

MATERIALS

Steel wire, 18 gauge (1 mm)

12 seed beads, size 6°, peach

12 flower buttons, 1 cm in diameter

24 silver crimp beads, ¹/8" (0.3 cm) in diameter

Branch of plastic leaves

Thin satin ribbon, pink, 10" (25 cm) in length

Silver pinback

Wire cutters

Superglue

Scissors

Flat-nose pliers

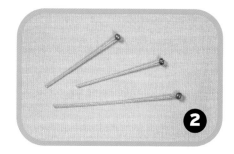

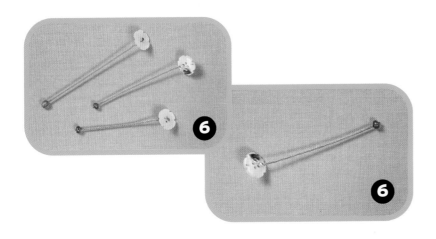

8. Tie the ends of the ribbon in a double knot and secure with drops of superglue.

6. Repeat Steps 4 and 5 to string all of the buttons onto the wires, securing each button with two crimp beads.

7. Gather together the wire stems to form a bouquet. Lay the plastic leaves under the wires, and lay the pinback behind the leaves. Wrap the ribbon securely around everything several times to secure.

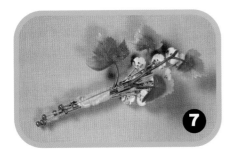

TWINKLING WREATH
BROOCH

The twinkling shank buttons I used in this brooch attract lots of attention—and plenty of curious looks. People wonder where I found such sparkly buttons; the fact that they are collected from generations of sweaters, shirts, and dresses is a secret I keep to myself.

Ready-Made Component

I never throw out **loose buttons**, especially if they are shiny, sparkly, or unusual. Single buttons whose original sources are unknown are easy to find—save them in a jar to make this fabulous brooch.
As for the ornament, it's **a classic Christmas ornament**—any shape or size will do.

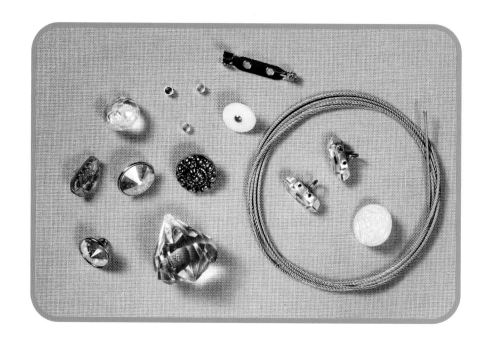

MATERIALS

Steel wire, 18 gauge (1 mm)

28 shiny shank buttons, various sizes

Crystal ornament, 1" (2.5 cm) in length

2 silver crimp beads

Silver pinback

Superglue

Strong sewing thread

Wire cutters

Flat-nose pliers

Sewing needle

INSTRUCTIONS

1. Cut a 12" (30.5 cm) piece of wire. String 14 buttons onto the wire, drawing them as close together as possible. Make sure the buttons don't slide off the other end of the wire.

2. String the ornament onto the wire, drawing along until it is flush with the buttons.

5. Draw the ends of the wire in opposite directions to make the buttons as crowded as possible. Mash the crimp beads with the flat-nose pliers. Make sure the beads are securely mashed as they are holding the circle together.

6. Thread the sewing needle with a comfortable length of thread, double it, and tie both ends together. Tie the thread to the pinback. Join the pinback to the wreath by wrapping the thread several times around the wire and the pinback. Tie the thread in a secure double knot and secure with drops of superglue.

3. String the remaining buttons onto the wire, then string two crimp beads.

4. Draw the ends of the wire together to form a wreath of buttons. String the second end through the crimp beads, forming an X of wire with the crimp beads at the center.

ACCESSORIES

MADAME BUTTERFLY'S
HAIR COMB

Though my kids were the ones who initiated the sticker craze in my house, it cannot be said that I didn't catch the fever. It's just so easy to make something nice a little bit nicer with a few stickers. Now I'm the sticker collector in the household—I pick up pretty flower stickers wherever I see them.

Ready-Made Component

Craft stores, toy stores, stationery stores, and office supply stores are all well stocked with stickers these days. **Elegant stickers** might be a little harder to find than cutesy ones, but they are available.

MATERIALS

11 stickers, floral motif

Metal hair comb, 2³/4" (7 cm) in length

20 roundhead fasteners, ¹/2" (1.3 cm) shank

Silver wire, 22 gauge (0.6 mm)

Lamination pouch

Laminator

Scissors

Awl

Wire cutters

INSTRUCTIONS

1. Arrange the stickers in a random fashion in the lamination pouch. Make sure the stickers aren't too close together.

2. Laminate the stickers using a home or industrial laminator.

3. Cut out the laminated stickers. Leave a ¹/8" (0.3 cm) margin around each sticker so that the lamination doesn't separate.

4. Punch holes in 2 stickers near their margins and connect with a fastener.

5. Punch another hole in one of the stickers you connected in Step 4. Punch a hole in a third sticker and connect the stickers with a fastener.

6. Continue connecting stickers in this manner until you have a strip of stickers that is long enough to cover the base of the comb.

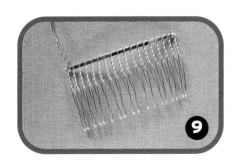

9. Wind the wire a few times around the base of the comb to secure in place.

10. Attach the stickers to the comb by winding the wire through the holes you made in Step 8 and around the base of the comb. Try to conceal the wire as much as possible.

7. Repeat Steps 4 to 6 to make 3 more strips of stickers.

8. Make several holes along one side of each strip of stickers.

JINGLE-JANGLE
COIN BELT

I'm not a serious coin collector—I usually just save coins for sentimental reasons. As for foreign coins, no matter how hard I try to empty my pockets from small change at the airport, I always seem to come home from trips abroad with a purse full of foreign change.

Ready-Made Components

This belt includes 36 **coins**; you can use any combination and denomination you like, including foreign coins, out-of-circulation coins, or freshly minted coins. As for the **bells**, miniature bells are easy to find at Christmas time, when many shops sell them along with wrapping paper and ornaments. Regarding the **chain**, you'll need to choose something with relatively large links for this belt, but make sure it isn't too heavy. You might want to test it out before you buy it by wrapping it around your hips a few times to make sure it hangs comfortably.

MATERIALS

29 wavy-edged silver coins

7 smooth-edged silver coins

8 silver bells, 1/2" (1.3 cm) in diameter

44 jump rings, 1/4" (0.6 cm) in diameter

2 pieces of silver link chain, 39" (100 cm) and 41" (105 cm) in length

Silver key ring

Drill with #60 (1 mm) drill bit
2 flat-nose pliers

INSTRUCTIONS

1. Drill a hole near the edge a coin and draw a jump ring through the hole.

2. Repeat Step 1 to prepare all of the coins.

2

3. Working with the shorter chain first, measure 4" (10 cm) from one end of the chain and attach a jump ring.

4. Link the two chains together by attaching the first link in the longer chain to the jump ring from Step 3.

5. Measure 4³/4" (12 cm) along the shorter chain from the point where the two chains are linked and attach a jump ring.

6. Measure 5³/4" (14.7 cm) along the longer chain from the point where the two chains are linked and attach the chain to the jump ring from Step 5.

7. Repeat Steps 5 and 6 to continue linking the chains together at regular intervals. The last link will be about 1³/4" (4.5 cm) from the end of the shorter chain.

8. Now you're ready to attach the coins. You'll be attaching coins to the longer chain first, so if you are using two types of coins, start with one of the 29 identical coins. Measure 2" (5 cm) from the point where the two chains are linked and attach a coin to the longer chain. Measure 1" (2.5 cm) and attach another coin. Measure 1" (2.5 cm) and attach another coin.

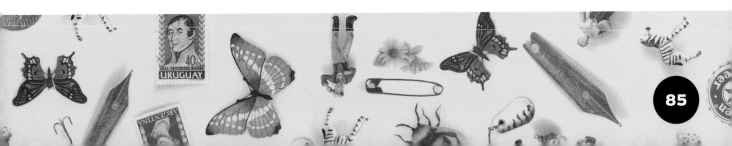

9. Repeat Step 8 another 6 times. Measure 2¹/₂" (5 cm) after the last coin and attach another coin.

10. Now you're ready to attach coins to the shorter chain. If you are using two types of coins, you'll be using the 7 identical coins for this. Measure 2³/₈" (6 cm) from the point where the two chains are linked and attach a coin.

11. Measure 4³/₄" (12 cm) from the coin you attached in Step 10 and attach another coin.

12. Repeat Step 11 another 5 times to attach the rest of the coins.

13. Attach a bell and one of the 29 identical coins to a jump ring that connects the two chains.

14. Repeat Step 13 to attach bells and coins to each of the jump rings connecting the two chains.

15. To finish, attach a jump ring to shorter end of the belt and attach the key ring.

HIP-HUGGING SAFETY
PIN **BELT**

Safety pins are one of the most ubiquitous devices in my life. I keep them stashed in kitchen cups, dresser drawers, purses, and coat pockets. Though I had to go beyond my personal supply to make this belt, it was inspired by the marvelous metal fasteners that have saved me from countless fallen hems, torn straps, and ripped seams over the years.

Ready-Made Component

Safety pins can be purchased in sewing stores, fabric stores, and hardware stores. The safety pins I used for this belt are 1½ " (3.8 cm) long, but they come in a wide range of sizes—make your belt wider or more narrow by choosing a different size safety pin.

MATERIALS

130 safety pins, 1¹/2" (3.8 cm) in length

900 seed beads, size 6°, various colors

50 glass beads, various sizes and colors

145 round beads, ¹/3" (0.9 cm) in diameter, various colors

Silver wire, 18 gauge (1 mm)

6 silver crimp beads, ¹/8" (0.3 cm) in diameter

1 silver jump ring, ¹/4" (0.6 cm) in diameter

Silver key ring

Wire cutters

2 flat-nose pliers

INSTRUCTIONS

1. Open a safety pin and string 7 to 9 seed beads onto the shank. Close the pin.

2. Repeat Step 1 to decorate 80 safety pins in this manner.

3. Open a safety pin and string 1 to 3 seed beads. String a glass bead then string a few more seed beads. Close the pin.

4. Repeat Step 3 to decorate 50 safety pins in this manner.

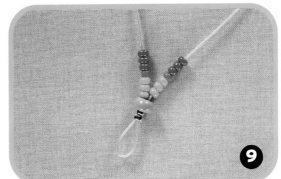

9

6

10. String a safety pin from Step 2 onto the wires by drawing one wire through the loop at the top of the pin and the other wire through the loop at the bottom of the pin. String a seed bead onto the top wire and a seed bead onto the bottom wire.

5. Cut a 78" (2 m) piece of wire and fold in half. String 2 crimp beads onto the folded end of the wire and draw along for about 1" (2.5 cm).

6. Mash the crimp beads with the flat-nose pliers to make a loop at this end of the wire.

7. String 1 round bead onto both wires at once.

8. String 3 yellow seed beads, 1 orange seed bead, and 3 red seed beads onto one of the wires.

9. Repeat Step 8 on the other wire.

11. Repeat Step 10 another 3 times, then string another safety pin from Step 2.

11

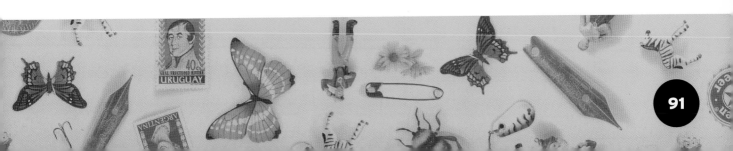

12. String a round bead onto the top wire and a round bead onto the bottom wire. String a safety pin from Step 4 onto the wires by drawing one wire through the loop at the top of the pin and the other wire through the loop at the bottom of the pin. String a round bead onto the top wire and a round bead onto the bottom wire.

13. Repeat Steps 10 to 12 another 8 times.

14. Repeat Step 12 another 32 times.

15. Repeat Steps 10 to 12 another 9 times.

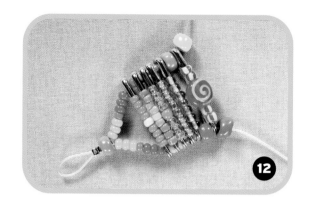

16. String 3 red seed beads and 2 crimp beads onto the top wire. String 3 red seed beads and 2 crimp beads onto the bottom wire.

17. Form a loop in each of the wires. Tuck the ends of the wires into the crimp beads and mash the crimp beads.

18. To finish, draw the jump ring through loops you made in Step 17 and attach the key ring to the jump ring.

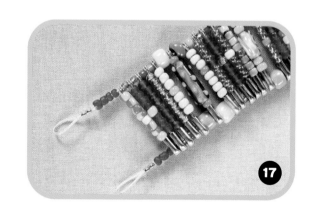

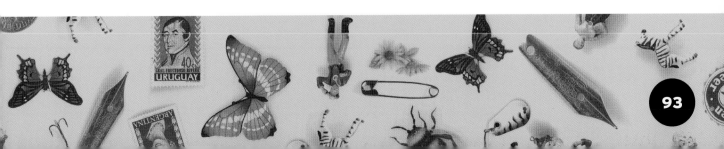

I'LL DRINK TO THAT!
HANDBAG CHARM

Bottle caps are a favorite keepsake in my household. Colorful and distinct, they are easy to collect; small and lightweight, they are easy to take home as souvenirs. They are also free (with the purchase of a beverage, of course).

Ready-Made Component

All you need to find enough **bottle caps** to make this necklace is a hot summer's day and a few bottles of your favorite soft drink or beer. True, bottled beverages often come with plastic caps these days, but many companies still bottle drinks the old-fashioned way—with shapely glass bottles and colorful metal caps.

MATERIALS

7 metal bottle caps, variety of brands

13 headpins, 1/2" (1.3 cm) in length

3 jump rings, 3/8" (0.9 cm) in diameter

Silver key ring

Permanent marker

Drill and #60 (1 mm) drill bit

Wire cutters

2 flat-nose pliers

Round-nose pliers

INSTRUCTIONS

1. Arrange the bottle caps in the shape of a flower and mark the points where the caps meet each other. You'll mark 6 equidistant points on the rim of the center cap and 3 points on the rims of the other caps—1 point where the cap meets the center cap and 2 points where it meets adjacent caps.

2. Drill holes in the areas you marked in Step 1.

3. Draw a headpin through a hole in the center bottle cap so that the head of the pin is on the inside of the cap. Insert this headpin into the middle hole of another cap.

4. Make a loop in the headpin and cut any excess wire.

5. Draw a headpin through an adjacent hole in the center bottle cap. Insert this headpin into the middle hole of another cap. Make a loop in the headpin and cut any excess wire.

6. Attach the outer bottle caps to each other by drawing a headpin through adjacent holes. Make a loop in the headpin and cut any excess wire.

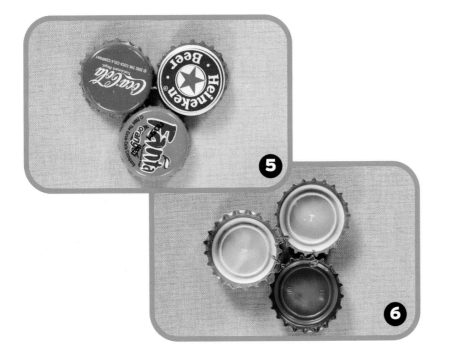

7. Repeat Steps 5 and 6 to attach 6 bottle caps to the center cap, and to each other. Attach the last cap to the first cap by drawing a headpin through adjacent holes. Make a loop in the headpin and cut any excess wire.

8. Drill a hole in the middle of the rim of one of the outer bottle caps. Draw a headpin through the hole so that the head of the pin is on the inside of the cap. Make a loop and trim any excess wire.

9. Connect the jump rings in a chain. Attach the jump ring at one end to the key ring.

10. Attach the jump ring at the other end to the headpin you attached in Step 9.

BUTTON-UP-THE-
EVENING **BAG**

I never throw out a button. Even if I don't remember where it came from, I save it. I have big buttons and little ones, plastic buttons and metal ones. I have 2-hole buttons, 4-hole buttons, and shank buttons. This project requires almost 200 buttons. Though I don't have this many matching buttons in my collection, it was inspired by the hundreds of mismatched buttons I have stored in glass jars and boxes.

Ready-Made Component

You'll find an endless selection of **buttons** at sewing stores and fabric stores. You can also find funky buttons at garage sales and bazaars, although it's unlikely you'll find 200 buttons that match. Be sure to choose 4-hole buttons for this project, as you'll be using all of the holes.

MATERIALS

192 4-hole silver buttons, 1/2" (1.3 cm) in diameter

400 silver jump rings, 2/5" (1 cm) in diameter

Thick satin fabric, smoky blue, 7 1/2" x 20" (19.8 cm x 51 cm)

Strong sewing thread

Embroidery floss, green

Thin satin ribbon, green, 28" (72 cm) in length

2 flat-nose pliers

Sewing needle

Embroidery needle

Scissors

INSTRUCTIONS

1. Connect 2 buttons by opening a jump ring and inserting each end into a button. Close the jump ring securely.

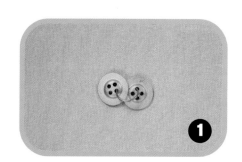

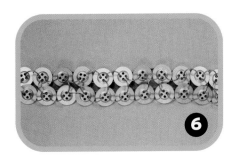

2. Open another jump ring and insert one end into the right hole of the button on the right. Insert the other end into another button and close the jump ring.

3. Continue connecting buttons in this manner until you have a chain of 12 buttons.

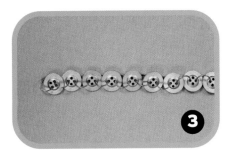

4. Repeat Steps 1 to 3 another 15 times to make 16 chains of buttons.

5. Draw one end of a jump ring through the bottom hole in the leftmost button on a chain. Draw the other end of the jump ring through the top hole in the leftmost button of another chain. Close the jump ring.

6. Continue joining the two chains of buttons in this manner.

7. Repeat Steps 5 and 6 until you have a sheet of buttons that is 12 buttons wide and 16 buttons high.

8. Fold the sheet of buttons in half to form a pocket that measures 12 buttons wide and 8 buttons high. Connect the sides of the pocket by drawing jump rings through the empty holes in adjacent buttons.

9. Thread the sewing needle with a comfortable length of thread, double it and tie both ends together.

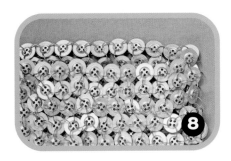

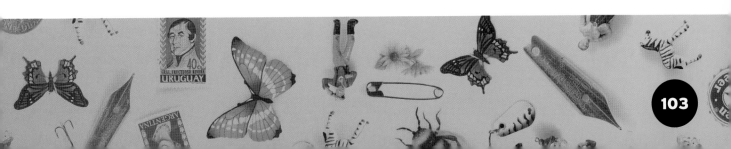

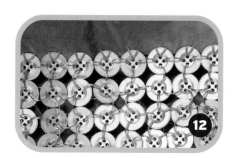

10. Fold the fabric in half with right-sides facing each other to form a pocket that measures 10" (25.5 cm) wide and 7¹/₂" (19.8 cm) high. Sew a running stitch along the sides and bottom of the pocket to make seams. Make a 1¹/₄" (3.2 cm) fold along the top of the pocket and sew the fold into place with a running stitch.

11. Thread the embroidery needle with a comfortable length of embroidery floss, double it and tie both ends together.

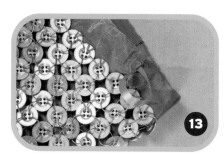

12. Press the fabric into the pocket of buttons. Attach the buttons to the fabric by sewing a stitch in each of the empty button holes along the top. Take care that the folded area at the top of the purse remains even all the way around.

13. To make the strap, push one end of the ribbon into one of the openings in the fold at the top of the purse. Draw the ribbon around until it comes out the other opening. You can attach a safety pin to the end of the ribbon to help you draw it through. Tie the ends of the ribbon in a secure double knot, then draw the ribbon backwards into the folded area of the purse to conceal the knot.

ZIPPER-A-DEE-DOO-DAH
PURSE

I consider zippers to be one of the greatest inventions of the 20th century. After all, can you imagine buttoning up a ski jacket when it's below zero? As for old jeans, I rarely throw them out. Not only do I love wearing them once they've been worked in (who doesn't?) but jean fabric is also incredibly durable.

Ready-Made Components

You can find **zippers** at any sewing or fabric store—choose bright or subdued colors, just be sure that the colors go well together. As for the **jean fabric,** any size or style of jeans will do—I recommend choosing a piece of fabric that has a pocket intact so it can function as a pocket in the purse, too.

MATERIALS

13 zippers, various shades of red, orange, and pink, 7³/4" (20 cm) in length

Jean fabric, 7³/4" x 10" (19.8 cm x 25.6 cm)

Thick ribbon, pink with white polka dots, 31" (80 cm) in length

15 tassels, various shades of orange, yellow, and red, 2¹/2" (6.4 cm) in length

Strong sewing thread, yellow, pink, and blue

Thick red strap, 39" (100 cm) in length

Sewing needle or sewing machine

Fabric scissors

INSTRUCTIONS

1. Lay 2 zippers side by side. Use the yellow thread to sew the zippers together with a running stitch.

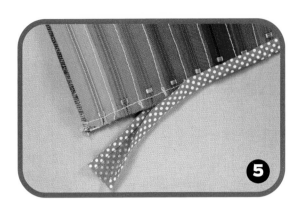

2. Lay a third zipper beside the pair from Step 1 and sew together with a running stitch. Continue sewing the zippers together in this manner to form a sheet of 13 zippers. Consider the order of the zippers in advance, so that the colors flow naturally.

3. Place the jean fabric wrong-side-up on your work surface. If there is a pocket on the fabric, make sure it's oriented toward the top of the fabric. Make a small fold along the top and sew a zigzag stitch along the edge using the yellow thread.

4. Place the sheet of zippers onto the jean fabric so that the wrong sides are touching. Sew the sides and bottom together with a running stitch, leaving the top open.

5. Fold the ribbon around the sewn edges of the purse so that it covers the seams. Sew into place with a running stitch using the pink thread.

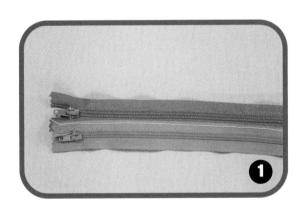

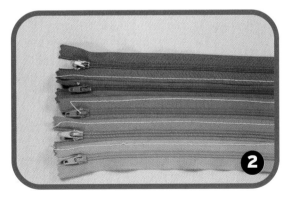

6. Sew together 3 tassels using the needle and thread.

7. Repeat Step 6 to make 4 more bunches of tassels.

8. Sew a bunch of tassels onto the bottom corner of the purse using the pink thread.

9. Measure 2" (5 cm) along the bottom and sew on another bunch of tassels.

10. Repeat Step 9 until all of the tassels are sewn onto the purse.

11. To finish, sew the ends of the strap onto the inside of the jean fabric with a running stitch using the blue thread.